Staveley Community Primary School
Staveley
North Yorkshire
HG5 9LQ
Tel 01423 340338
Headteacher Miss E E Miller

For Jesse

My bunny died last night

Barbara Smith
Illustrated by Rhian Nest James

paternoster
publishing

My bunny, Blackberry, died last night. We found her this morning lying quite still in her cage.

I cried and cried. My sister cried and cried and so did my little brother. I even cried at school and my friend comforted me. Later, I rang my grandma and she said, "You must try and think of all the happy times you had with Blackberry. She loved being with you."

Three years ago, my Gran had come with me to the farm to choose my bunny. I fell in love with Blackberry at first sight. She was small and fluffy with lop ears and a twitchy nose which made me laugh.

I carried her carefully home and put her in her brand new cage. I had saved my pocket money for ages to buy the best one I could for her and she snuggled down at once in the clean fresh hay I had put in her sleeping quarters.

Gran was right. We did have lots of happy times together. I remember when I found a book in the library which told me about the foods that rabbits liked best and Blackberry certainly liked her food. She grew rapidly!

She was adventurous too and after school I let her run in the garden. She loved to jump over obstacles that I constructed for her. We were friends and she knew I loved her.

Then one day
she was missing.
I found her cage
door wide open.

We searched
everywhere and
put a notice on
our gate. "Lost, one very much loved
black rabbit with lop ears and a twitchy
nose – reward given for finding her."
But no one came to collect it.

LOST

ONE VERY MUCH
LOVED BLACK RABBIT
WITH LOP EARS AND
A TWITCHY NOSE,
REWARD GIVEN
FOR FINDING HER

My mum rang the police station but no one had handed in a rabbit. Next day she rang the Animal Rescue Centre on the other side of town. A voice said, "We have a bunny here we've called Bad Bernadette. She was found in a car park near your home, she might be your bunny."

Mum bundled us all in the car and we drove to the Rescue Centre straight away. Bad Bernadette was *my* rabbit! I didn't scold her as she was so pleased to see me.

I think she'd wriggled in her cage at night
and the catch had come undone. Then
she'd hopped about looking for juicy
grass and could not find her way home.

I hugged her and hugged her and gave her
two carrots with her tea that night and
Dad fixed a new bolt on her cage.
Next day I wrote and
thanked the
lady who had
found her.

Now we have to bury Blackberry and I'm very sad. I don't like the idea of putting her under the ground but Mum says there are many things that are difficult to understand. Like how the seeds I planted last year became tall sunflowers and how the conker I buried is growing into a tree.

She says that when Blackberry is part of our garden, in some special way she will always be with us.

Copyright © 1997 Hunt & Thorpe

Text © 1997 Barbara Smith

Illustrations © 1997 Rhian Nest James

ISBN 1-85608-378-0

Designed by
THE BRIDGEWATER BOOK COMPANY LTD.

Write to:
Hunt & Thorpe
Laurel House, Station Approach, New Alresford,
Hampshire, SO24 9JH, UK

Hunt & Thorpe is a name used under licence by
Paternoster Publishing, PO Box 300,
Kingstown Broadway, Carlisle, CA3 0QS, UK

A CIP catalogue record for this book
is available from the British Library.

Printed in Hong Kong / China